For my Dad
– Z.T.

For my grandmother
– R.K.

Zoë Tucker is passionate about picture books and spends (almost) every day in the world of children's publishing. Working as an art director and designer, she has the opportunity to work with authors, artists, and publishers from all over the world. Zoë lives and works on the south coast of England, with her husband, Adam, and her cat, Murray, and she uses a computer (almost) every day! *Ada and the Number-Crunching Machine* is her debut as a picture book author.

Rachel Katstaller is an illustrator from tiny tropical El Salvador. After attending the Summer Residency in Illustration at the School of Visual Arts in New York City in 2014, Rachel decided to pursue her lifelong dream of becoming a children's book illustrator. Since then, Rachel has relocated to the Austrian Alps along with her cat, Hemingway.

Text copyright © 2019 by Zoë Tucker.

Illustrations copyright © 2019 by Rachel Katstaller.

First published in Switzerland under the title *Ada Lovelace und die Zahlen-Knack-Maschine*.

English text copyright © 2019 by NorthSouth Books, Inc., New York 10016.

First published in the United States, Great Britain, Canada, Australia, and New Zealand in 2019 by NorthSouth Books, Inc., an imprint of NordSüd Verlag AG, CH-8050 Zürich, Switzerland.

Distributed in the United States by NorthSouth Books, Inc., New York 10016.

Library of Congress Cataloging-in-Publication Data is available.

ISBN: 978-0-7358-4317-2 (trade edition)

1 3 5 7 9 • 10 8 6 4 2

Printed at Livonia Print, Riga, Latvia, March 2019

www.northsouth.com

Ada

and the
Number-Crunching
Machine

Written by
Zoë Tucker

illustrated by
Rachel Katstaller

This is Ada.

Now, Ada might *look* like
an ordinary little girl,
but the truth is
Ada changed the world.

Ada loved numbers
and solving problems.

Big problems, little problems,
and tricky complicated problems.

She read all the books in the library,
solved big sums, and invented crazy contraptions.

Ada was just like her mother, Annabella Milbanke,
who was very clever and spent her days studying math and
science and taking tea with the smartest people in London.
(She *also* read all the books in the library.)

Ada loved poetry and art.
She painted big messy pictures
and wrote very long letters.
She was wild and romantic,
bad-tempered and moody.

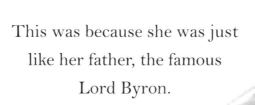

This was because she was just
like her father, the famous
Lord Byron.

Byron was brilliant with words and spent
his days roaming the country writing poetry.
(He was *also* quite bad-tempered, which
drove everyone around him crazy.)

· Lord Byron ·

In those days, little girls
like Ada didn't go to school.
This might sound like a wonderful plan,
but it was very, very boring. Young girls like Ada
were only expected to sing and dance, sew, paint and draw.

Ada was lucky.

Her mother believed that girls should have the same
opportunities as boys and so she found lots of bright people to
come and teach Ada in their home. The teachers brought maps of
far-off lands, star charts of the galaxy, plans for wild inventions
and amazing machines, lots of different animals, birds and
bugs to study, and beautiful plants to draw.

As you can imagine, Ada was a very good pupil, and as she
grew older, her teachers became her friends. Her best friend was
one Mr. Charles Babbage, an inventor and mathematical genius.
At the time, Charles was working on a fantastic new idea that
he couldn't wait to share with Ada.

One day a postcard arrived from Italy and it said:

My dear Ada,

Having a terrific time in Turin.
I've been telling people about a wonderful invention
I've been building.
It's a big counting machine that will solve the
longest sums you can imagine—an amazing number-
crunching mathematical masterpiece!
What do you think?
Wish you were here—the ice cream is very good
indeed.

Yours truly,
Charles

Taking his inspiration from the huge mechanical factories of the Industrial Revolution, Charles imagined a big machine with lots of moving parts. The machine would be fed with large cards, each punched through with a pattern of holes. These holes would tell the machine what to do.

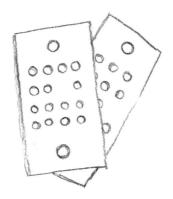

Ada thought this was a wonderful idea and immediately set to work. She began scribbling pages and pages of notes, swapping numbers for letters and then letters for symbols. Her brain was fizzing with excitement. If the machine could be told how to add up big sums, then maybe it could be told how to solve other problems too! Using her love of words and numbers, Ada wrote a special code that would tell the machine what to do.

They called it the Analytical Engine. And do you know what we call that machine today?

The computer!

Our world would be a very different place if it hadn't been for Ada and Charles and their invention. Their thoughts and ideas for the Amazing Number-Crunching Machine were the start of the very first computer, made more than 100 years later.

Ada changed our world. She was able to see things differently. She was clever, inventive, and creative, and she looked at problems from all angles. She was a true pioneer.

· ADA LOVELACE ·

Ada Lovelace (1815–1852) was a mathematician and computer engineer. She was born in London, on a cold December day, in 1815.

Things were different back then. Ada lived with her mother in a very smart part of town. There were no cars on the street, just horses and carriages rumbling by; and beyond the edge of the city, huge factories dotted the landscape, with big chimneys billowing steam. It was a time of Industrial Revolution.

Ada learned from Frend, Mary Somerville, and Augustus De Morgan. She was friends with Charles Dickens, Michael Faraday, and Andrew Crosse. She worked closely with Charles Babbage for many years and shared ideas and theories on his designs for the Analytical Engine.

In 1843 Ada was asked to translate an article by the Italian mathematician Luigi Menabrea. The article was all about Babbage's Analytical Engine. Because she knew so much about the machine already, Ada added her own notes to the translation—almost three times as many! Her notes included an algorithm (a code) that would give the machine instructions.

Ada predicted the Analytical Engine could do much more than number-crunching and one day it would be used to compose music, create pictures, and improve science. This all became true 100 years later. Her collaboration with Charles Babbage was the first step toward the computers we use today.

Ada is regarded as the world's first computer programmer. Her accomplishments made her a pioneer of not only mathematics, but of women in science. She is celebrated every year on the second Tuesday in October.

Charles Babbage (1791–1871) was a mathematician and inventor. In 1832 he designed his first counting machine, which he called the Difference Engine. He later went on to design the Difference Engine 2 and the Analytical Engine. They were so big, it would have taken years—and lots of money—to make them, so they were never fully built.

Fun facts:

- Ada Lovelace Day is recognized all over the world as a day to celebrate inspirational women in math, science, engineering, and technology. Its aim is to encourage and foster a future generation of Adas.
- The Ada Lovelace Awards are given every year by the Association of Women in Computers, to recognize outstanding achievements in technology.
- The United States Department of Defense named their computer language after Ada.
- Ada was crazy about machines and from a very early age enjoyed studying the designs for new mechanical inventions. Taking her inspiration from the great machines of the Industrial Revolution and the anatomy and mechanics of bird flight, Ada designed her own steam-powered flying machine. She was just twelve years old.
- Ada was a female pioneer in a man's world.
- At that time, it was believed that "overthinking" would cause madness in women! Throughout her lifetime, Ada published her works under her initials because women were considered not as clever as men.
- Ada was a musician as well as a scientist and regularly composed music. She dreamed that one day music notes could be replaced with numbers to make a code, and that these number codes could be used in the Analytical Engine to compose music.